A Kid's Guide to Drawing America™

How to Draw
West Virginia's
Sights and Symbols

Eric Fein

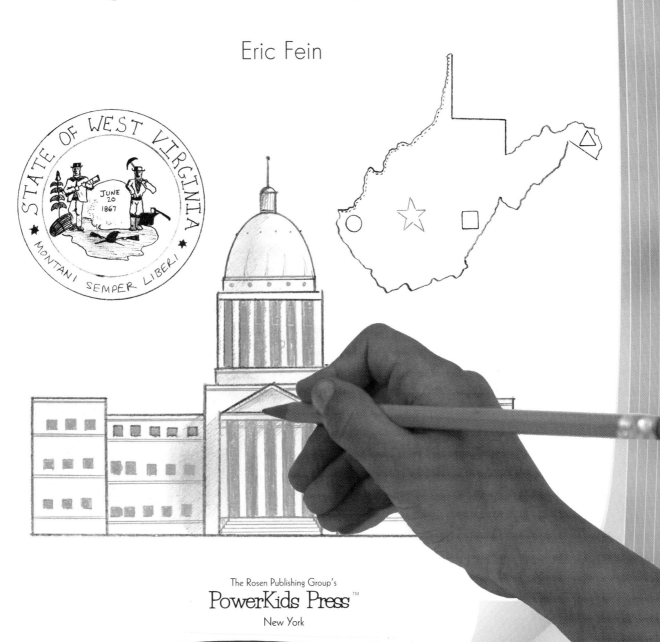

The Rosen Publishing Group's
PowerKids Press™
New York

Published in 2002 by The Rosen Publishing Group, Inc.
29 East 21st Street, New York, NY 10010

First Edition

Editor: Jennifer Way
Book Design: Kim Sonsky
Layout Design: Mike Donnellan

Illustration Credits: Jamie Grecco except p. 21 by Emily Muschinske.
Photo Credits: p. 7 © Michael Gadomski/Animals Animals; pp. 8–9 courtesy of Lillie Dawson Studios; pp. 12, 14 © One Mile Up, Incorporated; p. 16 Michael T. Sedam/CORBIS; p. 18 © Gary W. Carter/CORBIS; p. 20 © Robert Estall/CORBIS; p. 22 © Scott T. Smith/CORBIS; p. 24 © Bettmann/CORBIS; p. 26 © CORBIS; p. 28 © Richard T. Nowitz/CORBIS.

Fein, Eric
        How to draw West Virginia's sights and symbols / Eric Fein.
                p. cm. — (A kid's guide to drawing America)
        Includes index.
        Summary: This book explains how to draw some of West Virginia's sights and symbols, including the state seal, the official flower, and John Brown's Fort at Harpers Ferry.
        ISBN 0-8239-6105-2
        1. Emblems, State—West Virginia—Juvenile literature 2. West Virginia—In art—Juvenile literature 3. Drawing—Technique—Juvenile literature [1. Emblems, State—West Virginia 2. West Virginia 3. Drawing—Technique] I. Title II. Series
        743'.8'99754—dc21

Manufactured in the United States of America

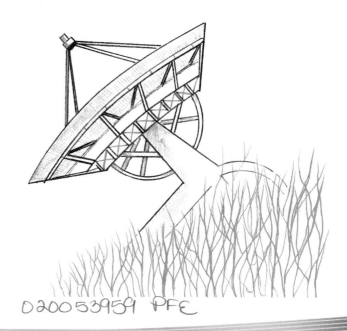

CONTENTS

Let's Draw West Virginia

West Virginia is located in some of the United States's most rugged land, the Appalachian Highlands. The state has many amazing places to see and things to do. The New River Gorge Bridges, near Fayette, West Virginia, are the world's longest steel arch span bridges. They are 1,700 feet (518 m) long and are the setting for Bridge Day. Every October people come to watch adventurers parachute and bungee jump from the bridges.

The Seneca Rocks are located in Pendleton County. They rise more than 900 feet (274 m) above the valley below. West Virginia is also home to one of the nation's oldest and largest Native American burial grounds. It is located in Moundsville, West Virginia. The Adena people built burial mounds, which are up to 69 feet high (21 m) and 900 feet (274 m) around at their base.

West Virginia's industries include coal mining, chemical and metal manufacturing, lumber, and glass products. Agriculturally the state produces poultry, eggs, cattle, dairy products, and apples.

This book will show you how to draw West Virginia's most interesting sights and symbols. In each chapter, there are step-by-step instructions that illustrate how to draw that chapter's subject. Every new drawing step will be highlighted in red. You will learn the names and the terms for the drawing shapes as you go along. To shade your drawings, tilt your pencil on its side and rub it from side to side.

You will need the following supplies to draw West Virginia's sights and symbols:

- A sketch pad
- An eraser
- A number 2 pencil
- A pencil sharpener

These are some of the shapes and drawing terms you need to know to draw West Virginia's sights and symbols:

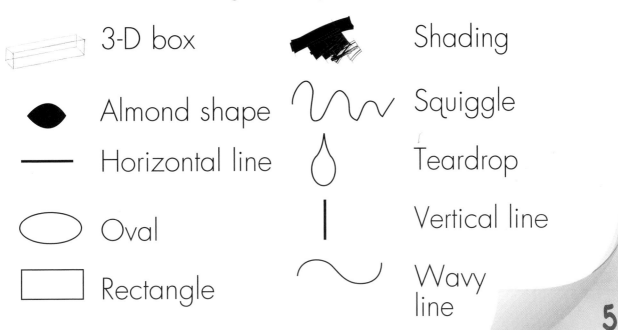

3-D box

Shading

Almond shape

Squiggle

Horizontal line

Teardrop

Oval

Vertical line

Rectangle

Wavy line

The Mountain State

West Virginia gets its nickname, the Mountain State, because it lies in the mountainous Appalachian Highlands. The first people to live in West Virginia were Native Americans called Early Hunters. They lived in the area more than 14,000 years ago. By the 1600s, the Native American population began to decrease due to diseases brought by white settlers.

During the 1800s, problems arose between eastern and western Virginia. Many people in eastern Virginia were slave owners who ran large plantations. Western Virginia was made up mostly of small family farms that did not use slave labor. Conflict about slavery reached a breaking point in 1859, when abolitionist John Brown and his followers attacked the arsenal in Harpers Ferry, West Virginia.

In 1861, western Virginians began to set up a government and a constitution separate from that of Virginia. West Virginia became the thirty-fifth state of the United States on June 20, 1863.

Each year the natural beauty of the Appalachian Highlands attracts many visitors. Seneca Rocks, in the Monogahela National Forest, is among the many popular camping and hiking destinations in West Virginia.

West Virginia Artist

Lillie Dawson

Lillie Dawson was born in 1951 in Charleston, West Virginia. Her mother encouraged her to take private art lessons when she was a child. Dawson took these lessons in Charleston. She then studied art at West Virginia Wesleyan College in Buckhannon.

Dawson prefers to paint landscapes and flowers. Sometimes she does abstract paintings, too. Abstract paintings do not have a recognizable subject, but instead focus on things such as color, shape, or mood.

Dawson started out painting in oil paints and in acrylic paints. She soon discovered watercolor paints and fell in love with them. Watercolors give an artist more choices in how to paint. The artist can begin with the paint dark and thick. Then, by wetting the brush, the artist can thin out the paint to make the color lighter. Mistakes made in watercolor are difficult to cover up by using more paint, though. With acrylic or oil paints, covering mistakes is much easier.

Dawson has painted many landscapes of West Virginia. Her painting *The Hokes Mill Bridge* is a picture of a covered bridge that is still in use. The house in *The Old Home Place* used to be her family's home. It was torn down in 1947.

This house in Dawson's 1982 painting *The Old Home Place* once stood near Sissonville, West Virginia. This watercolor measures 15" x 21" (38 cm x 53 cm).

Map of West Virginia

Map of the Continental United States

West Virginia takes up an area of 24,231 square miles (62,758 sq km). West Virginia is bordered by five states. Pennsylvania and Maryland lie to the north. Virginia borders the east and the south. Kentucky and Ohio border the west. Major rivers in West Virginia include the Potomac, the Kanawha, the Shenandoah, and the Ohio.

There are two main regions in West Virginia, the Appalachian Ridge and Valley region and the Appalachian Plateau. The Appalachian Ridge and Valley region runs along the state's eastern border. The Appalachian Plateau is farther to the west and is known for its narrow valleys carved by streams.

1

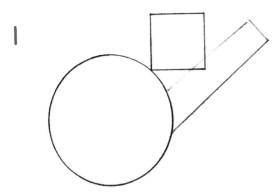

To draw West Virginia, begin by drawing a rectangle, a square, and a circle. These shapes will be your guides for the drawing.

2

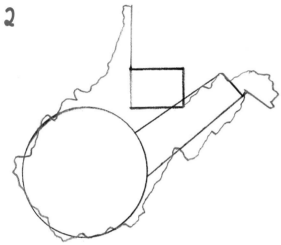

Using your guides, draw the shape of West Virginia. These lines are crooked, so pay close attention to the picture as you draw.

3

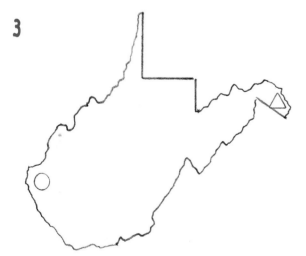

Erase extra lines. Now you have West Virginia's shape. Draw a circle for Huntington. Add a triangle to mark Harpers Ferry.

4

Draw a square to mark the Allegheny Plateau and a dotted line for the Ohio River.

5

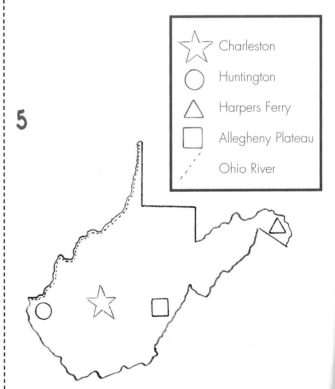

☆ Charleston
○ Huntington
△ Harpers Ferry
□ Allegheny Plateau
⌒ Ohio River

To finish your map, draw a star to mark Charleston, the capital of West Virginia. You can also make a key for your map.

The State Seal

West Virginia's state seal was designed by Joseph H. Diss Debar. He was an artist from Doddridge County, West Virginia. He was chosen by a legislative committee to render, or draw, the state seal. The Great Seal of West Virginia was adopted on September 26, 1863.

The seal features the state's motto, *Montani Semper Liberi*, which is Latin for "mountaineers are always free." At the top of the seal are the words "State of West Virginia." A farmer and a miner stand on either side of a large rock carved with June 20, 1863, the date of West Virginia's admittance into the United States.

The seal also has a design on the reverse side. This design shows a log house, hills, factories, and boats.

1

Begin drawing the seal by making a circle. Draw another circle inside the first circle. Then add two small ovals in the inner circle. These will become the heads of the farmer and the miner.

2

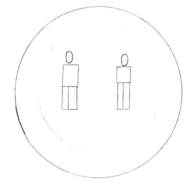

Add rectangles for the bodies and the legs.

3

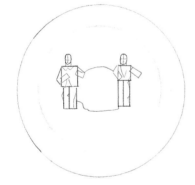

Add the stone in the center by drawing a rounded rectangle. Draw arms using thin rectangles. Add detail to the men's faces and bodies.

4

Add clothes and detail to the farmer and the miner. Erase extra lines.

5

Draw tools, a stalk of corn, and a bale of hay. Make an outline of the ground using a wavy line.

6

Write the words "STATE OF WEST VIRGINIA" and "MONTANI SEMPER LIBERI" around the edge of the seal. Write the date JUNE 20 1867 on the stone. Add shading and detail and you're done.

The State Flag

On March 7, 1929, West Virginia's legislature adopted the current state flag. The flag uses the state coat of arms, which is the image that appears on the state seal. The coat of arms rests on a white background and has a blue border. A wreath of rhododendrons encircles the coat of arms. Above this is a ribbon that reads "State of West Virginia."

Like the seal, the flag shows the farmer and the miner. The farmer represents agriculture and the miner represents industry. In front of the rock are two rifles and a Phrygian cap. In ancient Rome, the Phrygian cap represented a person that had been freed from slavery. The cap and the rifles symbolize that West Virginia is ready and willing to fight for freedom.

1

Begin by drawing a rectangle. Add another rectangle inside the first one.

2

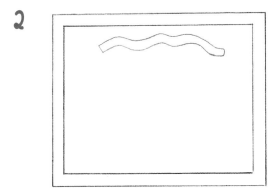

Add a wavy shape near the top of the inside rectangle. This will be the flag's banner.

3

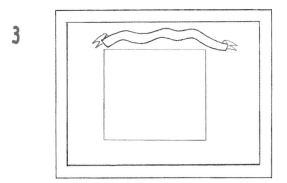

Finish the banner using curved shapes on either end. Make a rectangle for the shape of the crest.

4

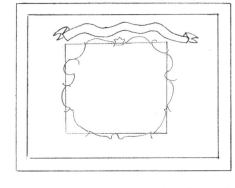

Using the rectangle as a guide, draw the basic shape of the crest, using curvy lines.

5

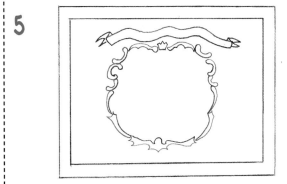

Finish the outline of the crest using wavy lines. Erase extra lines.

6

Add the words "STATE OF WEST VIRGINIA" to the banner. To draw the details of the crest, refer to the drawing instructions for the state seal on page 13. Add detail and shading, and you're done.

The Rhododendron

The rhododendron (*Rhododendron maximum*) is also known as the big laurel. In 1901, West Virginia's governor, George Atkinson, announced to the people of the state that they should pick an official flower. He suggested the rhododendron. He thought that the rhododendron was a good choice because it grows all over the state and is "admired both for its beauty and fragrance."

In 1902, West Virginia's schoolchildren voted on a state flower. The rhododendron got 19,000 votes out of a total of 36,000. The rhododendron became West Virginia's official state flower on January 23, 1903.

1

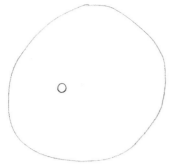

Begin by making a large, circular shape that will be your guide for drawing the rhododendron. Add a small circle. This is the center of one of the flowers.

2

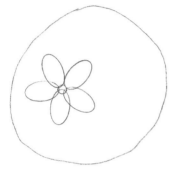

Add five ovals around the center for petals.

3

Using the ovals as guides, draw in the shape of the petals using wavy lines. You've made one of the many flowers that grow in clusters on the rhododendron.

4

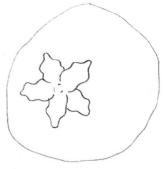

Erase extra lines.

5

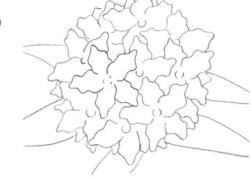

Repeat steps one through four until you've filled in the guide circle. Erase the guide circle. Add the plant's leaves along each side.

6

Add shading and detail to your flower, and you're done.

The Cardinal

The cardinal (*Cardinalis cardinalis*) was made West Virginia's state bird on March 7, 1949. The cardinal was chosen in a vote taken by schoolchildren.

A female cardinal usually lays three or four eggs. She sits on them until they hatch 12 or 13 days later. During this time, the male cardinal brings food back to the nest. At first both parents feed the young. The mother soon flies off to set up the next nest. Young cardinals leave their nest about 10 days after they are born.

Cardinals eat seeds, wild fruit, grain, worms, beetles, and other insects. Cardinals are also known to eat raisins, apples, and even bread!

1

To draw the cardinal, begin by drawing three circles for the rough shape of the bird.

2

Connect your circles to form the shape of the bird's body.

3

Add two triangles, one for the beak and one for the head feathers. Also add a dot for the eye.

4

Erase extra lines. Add two triangles, one for the wing, and one for the tail.

5

Erase extra lines and draw the legs and the feet. Add a thin, curvy shape for the perch, or branch.

6

Add shading and detail to your bird, and you're done. You can also smudge your lines to make the shading more effective.

The Sugar Maple

The sugar maple (*Acer saccharum*) was named West Virginia's official state tree on March 7, 1949. Sugar maples have many branches covered with leaves.

In the fall, the maple's leaves change color. They turn bright red, orange, and yellow. The wood of a sugar maple is very hard and is used for making furniture and musical instruments, such as violins.

Sugar maple trees have liquid inside them called sap. Sap is collected in the spring. The sap begins to flow inside the tree when the temperature is above 32°F (0°C). Special tools drill into the trunk of the maples to get the sap. The sap is then boiled down and turned into delicious maple syrup.

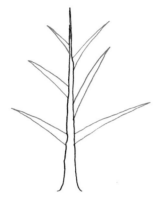

Begin by drawing a long trunk. Notice how the trunk becomes thin at the top. Use wiggly lines, because the surface of the bark is rough.

2

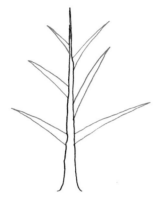

Add branches. Use the same shape as the one you used to make the trunk to make the branches.

3

Draw smaller branches growing out of the larger ones.

4

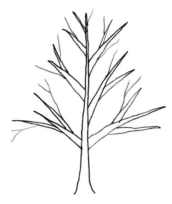

Add twiglike branches. Use wiggly lines.

5

Draw the outline of the fluffy, leafy top of the tree.

6

You don't need to draw each leaf. Instead shade the tree using scribbly lines. This will create the look of the leaves.

The Reber Radio Telescope

The Reber Radio Telescope was designed by Grote Reber, an engineer. It is the first instrument designed to find radio waves in space.

Radio telescopes collect radio waves from space. The Sun is one source of radio waves. Radio telescopes use a large dish antenna to collect these radio waves.

The telescope measures 31 feet (9.5 m) around and is made from 72 wooden radial, or raylike, rafters. These rafters are covered with a skin made of steel.

In the 1960s, Reber donated his telescope to the National Radio Astronomy Observatory (NRAO), a scientific organization in Green Bank, West Virginia. The NRAO at Green Bank offers tours to the public.

1

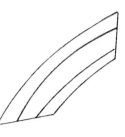

Start by drawing the curved shape of the dish.

2

Add three triangles with two rectangles at the peak. This is the antenna of the satellite.

3

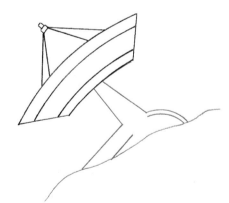

Draw the base, then add in a rough tree line at the bottom.

4

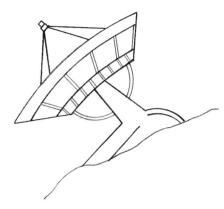

Draw two curved shapes for the supports of the dish. Add thin rectangles for the dish's details.

5

Add more lines to complete the dish. Draw wavy lines for tree branches.

6

Finish the tree branches. Add detail and shading, and you're done.

The B&O Railroad

The Baltimore & Ohio (B&O) Railroad Company created the first railway system in the United States. The project was done in Baltimore, because it had a large Atlantic port. This made it easier to get goods that came off of ships to the trains.

In the 1840s, the B&O railroad reached the area that would become West Virginia. It ran through Martinsburg, West Virginia. This city then grew.

Although trains and stations were damaged during the Civil War (1861–1865), the B&O Railroad Company continued to develop and to expand.

Today there is a restored B&O roundhouse in Martinsburg, where the Railroad Days Festival is held every July.

1

Start by drawing a circle for the main wheel of the train and a straight line for the track.

2

Add seven smaller circles for the other wheels.

3

Draw four rectangles for the train cars.

4

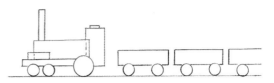

Erase extra lines. Make five more rectangles for the train's engine.

5

Draw the top of the smokestack using a triangle. Add cargo using rectangles and a curved line.

6

Add smoke coming from the smokestack. Add detail and shading, and you're done.

John Brown's Fort at Harpers Ferry

John Brown was an abolitionist. An abolitionist is someone who wants to end slavery. On October 16, 1859, Brown and 21 followers raided the federal arsenal in Harpers Ferry, in today's eastern West Virginia. Brown wanted to use the weapons inside to arm slaves so they could revolt against slavery. Brown and his followers were soon captured and were convicted of treason.

The building that became known as John Brown's Fort was a small guardhouse near the arsenal. Brown and his followers had barricaded themselves inside this building. The National Park Service bought the building in 1960.

No. 30. John Brown's Fort, Harper's Ferry

1

Begin drawing John Brown's Fort by making two long rectangles, and two slanted rectangles for the side of the fort. This will give your drawing a three-dimensional look.

2

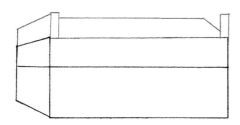

Add three rectangles for the roof. The fourth shape, in the center, looks like a rectangle with a corner cut off.

3

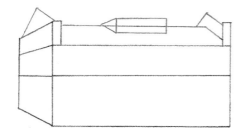

Add triangle shapes for the roof's peaks, and a triangle and a rectangle at the center of the roof.

4

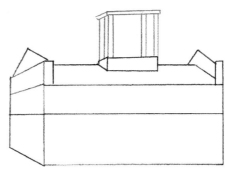

Erase extra lines. Add six thin rectangles to finish the structure at the center of the roof.

5

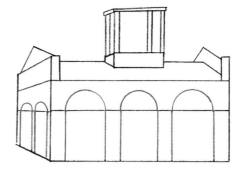

Draw three curved shapes along the front, and two curved shapes along the side of the fort.

6

Write the words "JOHN BROWN'S FORT" along the front of the building, over the doors. Add shading and detail to your building, and you're done.

West Virginia's Capitol

West Virginia's first state capital was in Wheeling. The capital was changed several times. After a vote in 1877, Charleston became West Virginia's permanent capital.

The fourth capitol building to be built in Charleston burnt down in 1921. Cass Gilbert, a famous architect, was chosen to design a new capitol. He had designed capitol buildings for Minnesota and for Arkansas. He also designed the Woolworth Building in New York City.

West Virginia's capitol takes up more than 16 acres (6 ha). It took eight years to build, and it was completed in 1932.

1

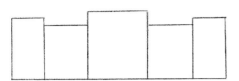

Begin drawing the capitol by making five rectangles, noting their size and their placement on the page.

2

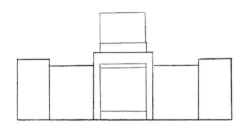

Make two rectangles on the top of the center rectangle. This will form the base of the dome. Add three rectangles in the center rectangle.

3

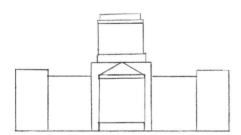

Draw two more rectangle on the dome's base. Add a triangle on the center rectangle.

4

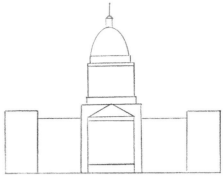

Add a half oval for the dome. Make the shape on the top of the dome. This is called a cupola. Add a line coming out of the top of the cupola.

5

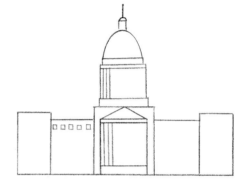

Finish the dome's base with many vertical lines. Add columns to the front of the building. Begin drawing windows using small squares.

6

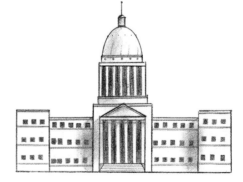

Finish drawing the columns and the windows. Add shading and detail to your building, and you're done.

West Virginia Facts

Statehood	June 20, 1863, 35th state
Area	24,231 square miles (62,758 sq km)
Population	1,811,000
Capital	Charleston, population, 56,100
Most Populated City	Charleston
Industries	Coal mining, chemical and metal manufacturing, glass products
Agriculture	Tobacco, poultry, eggs, cattle, apples
Animal	Black bear
Songs	"The West Virginia Hills," "This is My West Virginia," "West Virginia, My Home Sweet Home"
Bird	Cardinal
Flower	Rhododendron
Tree	Sugar maple
Fish	Brook trout
Motto	*Montani Semper Liberi*, Mountaineers Are Always Free
Insect	Monarch butterfly
Nickname	The Mountain State

Glossary

abolitionist (a-buh-LIH-shun-ist) Someone who worked to end slavery.

architecture (AR-kih-tek-chur) The science, art, or profession of designing buildings.

arsenal (AR-sih-nul) A storehouse of weapons.

astronomy (uh-STRAH-nuh-mee) The study of objects and matter outside Earth's atmosphere and of their physical and chemical properties.

barricaded (BAR-uh-kayd-ed) To have locked oneself inside a room or a building.

Civil War (SIH-vul WOR) The war fought between the northern and southern states of America from 1861 to 1865.

cupola (KYOO-puh-luh) A small structure built on a roof.

legislature (LEH-jihs-lay-cher) A body of people that has the power to make or pass laws.

motto (MAH-toh) A short sentence or phrase that says what someone believes or what something stands for.

observatory (ob-ZER-vuh-tor-ee) A building or a place equipped for the study of astronomy.

Phrygian (FRIH-jee-en) Of or related to Phrygia, an ancient, extinct area in Indo-Europe.

plantations (plan-TAY-shunz) Very large farms where crops are grown.

plateau (pla-TOH) A flat area of land.

revolt (rih-VOLT) To fight or rebel.

roundhouse (ROWND-hows) A circular building in which railroad locomotives are stored or are repaired, consisting of a central turntable with several sections of track coming from it.

Index

Web Sites

To learn more about West Virginia, check out these Web sites:
www.50states.com/wvirgini.htm
www.state.wv.us